797,885 Books

are available to read at

www.ForgottenBooks.com

Forgotten Books' App
Available for mobile, tablet & eReader

ISBN 978-1-330-24940-6
PIBN 10000795

This book is a reproduction of an important historical work. Forgotten Books uses
state-of-the-art technology to digitally reconstruct the work, preserving the original format
whilst repairing imperfections present in the aged copy. In rare cases, an imperfection in
the original, such as a blemish or missing page, may be replicated in our edition. We do,
however, repair the vast majority of imperfections successfully; any imperfections that
remain are intentionally left to preserve the state of such historical works.

Forgotten Books is a registered trademark of FB &c Ltd.
Copyright © 2015 FB &c Ltd.
FB &c Ltd, Dalton House, 60 Windsor Avenue, London, SW19 2RR.
Company number 08720141. Registered in England and Wales.

For support please visit www.forgottenbooks.com

1 MONTH OF FREE READING

at

www.ForgottenBooks.com

By purchasing this book you are eligible for one month membership to ForgottenBooks.com, giving you unlimited access to our entire collection of over 700,000 titles via our web site and mobile apps.

To claim your free month visit:

www.forgottenbooks.com/free795

* Offer is valid for 45 days from date of purchase. Terms and conditions apply.

Similar Books Are Available from
www.forgottenbooks.com

The Art of Being Alive
Success Through Thought, by Ella Wheeler Wilcox

Ethics of Success
by William Makepeace Thayer

How to Make Money
Three Lectures on "The Laws of Financial Success", by B. F. Austin

Success
by Ralph Waldo Emerson

Successful Business-Men
Short Accounts of the Rise of Famous Firms, by Alexander H. Japp

The Science and Art of Selling
by James Samuel Knox

Developing Executive Ability
by Enoch Burton Gowin

The Manual of Successful Storekeeping
by William Rowland Hotchkin

Increasing Human Efficiency in Business
A Contribution to the Psychology of Business, by Walter Dill Scott

Entering New Businesses
Selecting the Strategies for Success, by Charles A. Berry

The Psychology of Selling Life Insurance
by Edward K. Strong

Making Good in Business
by Roger W. Babson

Business Philosophy
by Benjamin Franklin Cobb

Loyalty in Business
And One and Twenty Other Good Things, by Elbert Hubbard

Salesmanship and Business Efficiency
by James Samuel Knox

The Ambitious Woman in Business
by Eleanor Gilbert

The Successful Salesman
by Frank Farrington

Brief Counsels Concerning Business
by An Old Man Of Business

The Business Life
Or Straight Talks on Business, by William Gamble

Personality in Business
by Andrew Carnegie

LECTURES ON BUSINESS EFFICIENCY
Edited by THOMAS H. RUSSELL, A.M., LL. D.

BUSINESS

By
ANDREW CARNEGIE

UNIVERSITY of CALIFORNIA
AT
LOS ANGELES
LIBRARY

UNIV. OF CALIFORNIA
AT LOS ANGELES LIBRARY

COPYRIGHT 1916 BY

WHITMAN PUBLISHING CO.

RACINE   CHICAGO

UNIV. OF CALIFORNIA
AT LOS ANGELES LIBRARY

INTRODUCTION

No apology is needed for presenting this famous lecture very early in this series for the perusal of business students. Rather may we congratulate ourselves and our readers on the privilege we have of using and studying Mr. Carnegie's words of practical wisdom. For there is a world of wisdom in what he has to say to young men about their careers and their conduct in business life.

Mr. Carnegie occupies a unique position in American business history. He is the one American business man par excellence who has shown us how to retire from business gracefully and enjoy life in retirement. In this he has set an example worthy of emulation. For there is nothing more absurd in the business creed than the belief quite commonly accepted that a business man should "die in the harness" and that no man can be happy in retirement after an active business life. The trouble is that few men know how to retire gracefully and happily, because they have not prepared themselves by cultivation of the mind for congenial occupation of their leisure by avocations—call them hobbies, if you will—that serve as a substitute for the cares and responsibilities of business.

In his retirement Mr. Carnegie is well employed, and the world has been enriched by his career both before and since he retired from active participation in the great steel industry. He divides his time nowadays between his native land and the country of his adoption, in which he gained his wealth and lasting fame. He came to this country a poor boy, having borrowed the money for his passage from Scotland. He toiled hard for his start in business and made his money largely by his wonderful judgment of men and skill in the selection of his lieutenants. Many of these—

young men too—became millionaires under his leadership, and some of them remain today at the top of the ladder of American industry But Mr. Carnegie worked and worked hard. His life has long been an open book to the American public, and few there are who do not wish the "Laird of Skibo" well in the happy enjoyment of his remaining years on the Scottish estate near the humble home of his youth, where his success is an inspiration to every young man and the most notable example of the opportunities afforded by business life in America.

Every word of Mr. Carnegie's lecture is worth study. He speaks out of a ripe experience to young men, with a heart brimful of kindness and human sympathy. He shows the steps that must be mounted in a regular advance to business success, and insists that there is no lack of opportunities today for those who learn how to find them or to make them. He advocates the business career for young men rather than artistic or professional careers, for reasons that to an open mind are good and convincing, and commends it as the one vocation in which "there is abundant room for the exercise of man's highest power and of every good quality in human nature."

I have never had any patience with those who spend their time envying the successful rich, especially when the envied rich man was once a poor young man and made his way in the world by his own efforts in legitimate business. To the envious I would say: The road is open to you, as it was to them; go thou and do likewise! And I commend the example of Andrew Carnegie in his business life to all young men entering business, as I commend his example in retirement to business men who lack the ability to retire. Both classes will find food for thought in this lecture.

T. H. R.

Business

By ANDREW CARNEGIE

Business is a large word, and in its primary meaning covers the whole range of man's efforts. It is the business of the preacher to preach, of the physician to practice, of the poet to write, the business of the university professor to teach, and the business of the college student, one might sometimes think, from the amount of attention bestowed upon it, to play football. I am not to speak of "business" in this wide sense, but specifically as defined in the Century Dictionary:

> "Mercantile and manufacturing pursuits collectively; employment requiring knowledge of accounts and financial methods; the occupation of conducting trade; or monetary transactions of any kind."

The illustration which follows is significant, and clearly defines this view of business. It reads:

> "It seldom happens that men of a studious turn acquire any degree of reputation for their knowledge of business."

But we must go one step further, more strictly to define business, as I am to consider it. Is a railway president receiving a salary, or the president of a bank, or a salaried officer of any kind, in business? Strictly speaking, he is not; for a man, to be in business, must be at least part owner of the enterprise which he manages and to which he gives his attention, and chiefly dependent for his revenues not upon salary but upon its profits. This view rules out the entire salaried class. None of these men are now men in business, but many of them have been, and most successful therein. The business man pure and simple plunges into and tosses upon the waves of human affairs without a life-preserver in the shape of salary; he risks all.

Choice of a Career.

There is no fortune to come from salary, however high, and the business man pursues fortune. If he be wise he puts all his eggs in one basket, and then watches that basket. If he is a merchant in coffee, he attends to coffee; if a merchant in sugar, he attents to sugar and lets coffee alone, and only mixes them when he drinks his coffee with sugar in it. If he mine coal and sell it, he attends to black diamonds; if he own and sail ships, he attends to shipping, and he ceases to insure his own ships just as soon as he has surplus capital and can stand the loss of one without imperiling solvency; if he manufacture steel, he sticks to steel, and severely lets copper alone; if he mine iron-stone, he sticks to that, and avoids every other kind of mining, silver and gold-mining especially. This is because a man can thoroughly master only one business and only an able man can do this. I have never yet met the man who fully understood two different kinds of business; you cannot find him any sooner than you can find a man who thinks in two languages equally and does not invariably think only in one.

Subdivision, specialization, is the order of the day.

Every Man to His Trade or His Specialty.

I have before me many representatives of all classes of students. If I could look into your hearts, I should find many different ambitions; some aiming at distinction in each of the professions; some would be lawyers, some ministers, some doctors, some architects, some electricians, some engineers, some teachers, and each sets before him, as models, honored names that have reached the highcst rank in these professions. The embryo lawyers before me would rival Marshall and Story of the past, or Carter and Choate of the present; the preacher would be a Brooks or a Van Dyke; the physician a Janeway or a Garmany; the editor would be a Dana; the architect a Richardson, and, having reached the top of his darling profession, his ambition then would be satisfied. At least, so he thinks at present. With these classes I have nothing whatever to do directly today, because all these are professional enthusiasts. Nevertheless, the qualities essential for success in the professions being in the main the same which insure success in business, much that I have to say applies equally to you all.

There remain among you those who would sail the uncertain sea of business, and devote themselves to making money, a great fortune, so that you shall be millionaires. I am sure that while this may be chiefly in your thoughts, it is not all you seek in a business career; you feel that in it there is scope for exercise of great abilities, of enterprise, energy, judgment, and all the best traits of human nature, and also that men in business perform useful service to society.

I am to try to shed a little light upon the path to success, to point out some of the rocks and shoals in that treacherous sea, and give a few hints as to the mode of sailing your ship, or rowing your shell, whether, for instance, the quick or the slow stroke is surer to win in the long race.

The Start in Life.

Let us begin, then, at the beginning. Is any would-be business man before me content in forecasting his future, to figure himself as laboring all his life for a fixed salary? Not one, I am sure. In this you have the dividing line between business and non-business; the one is a master, and depends upon profits, the other a servant, and depends upon salary. Of course, you have all to begin as servants with salary, but you have not all to end there.

You have some difficulty in obtaining a start, great difficulty as a rule, but here comes in the exceptional student. There is not much difficulty for him; he has attracted the attention of his teachers who know many men of affairs; has taken prizes; he is head of his class; has shown unusual ability, founded upon characteristics which are sure to tell in the race; he has proved himself self-respecting, has irreproachable habits, good sense, method, untiring industry, and his spare hours are spent in pursuing knowledge, that being the labor in which he most delights.

One vital point more; his finances are always sound, he rigorously lives within his means, and last, but not least, he has shown that his heart is in his work. Besides all this, he has usually one strong guarantee of future industry and ambitious usefulness, he is not burdened with wealth; it is necessary that he make his own way in the world. He is not yet a millionaire, but is only going to be one. He has no rich father, or, still more dangerous, rich mother, who can, and will, support him in idleness should he prove a failure; he has no life-preserver, and therefore must sink or swim. Before that young man leaves college he is a marked man. More than one avenue is open for him. The door opens before he is ready to knock; he is waited for by the sagacious employer. Not the written certificate of his professor, for certificates have generally to be read, and are read within the lines; but a word or two spoken to the business man who is always on the lookout for the exceptional young graduate, has secured the young man all that a young man needs—a start. The most valuable acquisition to his business which an employer can obtain is an exceptional young man; there is no bargain so fruitful for him as this.

It is, of course, much more difficult for only the average student; he has generally to search for employment, but finally he also gets a start.

Openings to Success.

The career of the exceptional student illustrates the path way to success. We need not render ourselves anxious about him; he is all right. He has been thrown into the sea, but he does not need any life-preserver; he does not need to be coddled, he will swim; he was not born to be drowned, and you see him breast the waves year after year until he is at the head of a great business. His start, of course, is not at the head, he is at the foot; fortunately so, for that is the reason his progress has always been upward. If he had started high he would not have had the chance to make a continual ascent. It does not matter much how he starts, for the qualities in him are such as to produce certain effects in any field he enters. He goes forward upon a very small salary, performing certain small uses, indeed, much smaller than he thinks himself capable of performing, but these he performs thoroughly.

Some day in some way something happens that brings him to the notice of his immediate superior. He objects to some plan proposed, and thinks it can be bettered in some way, or he volunteers to assist in a department other than his own; or he stops, one day, later at his work than usual, or goes some morning sooner, because there was some part of the business that had not been entirely settled the night before, or there was something to start next morning that he was afraid might not be ready or just right, and he "just goes down early that morning and finds his salaried young man, showing that he does not work for salary alone; it is not solely an affair of "hire and salary" with him; he is not that kind of a young man; he is working for the success of the business. Or it may be that some day his employer' proposes a certain mode of action in regard to a customer's account; perhaps the young man has started the credits, a most important part. His employers wish to close this credit, which, perhaps would embarrass the customer. This young man, known to the customer, had had to visit his place occasionally in the course of business, collecting his accounts, or trying to collect them, and the young man modestly says he is a splendid fellow, bound to succeed, does his business upon fair and wise methods, and only needs a little temporary indulgence to come out all right.

The employer has faith in the young man's judgment and ability, thinks it a rather strong suggestion for a clerk to make, but says to him: "You look out for this matter, and see that we do not lose, but, of course, we do not wish to injure one of our customers; if we can help him without risk we wish to do it." The young man takes the matter in hand, and results prove he was quite right; the customer becomes one of the very best of all their customers, and one that it would require a great deal to take away from the firm.

Or, perhaps, the bright young man may have noted the insurance policies upon the works, and their dates of expiration; he finds the fact has been overlooked—that some of the insurances have lapsed and are invalid. It is none of his business; he is not paid to look after the insurance of the firm; in one sense—the narrow sense—that is the business of some other man, but he ventures to call attention to the fact, and suggests that the premiums should be paid. But, now mark the advantage of general reading and education. This young man has read the newspapers and reviews, and learns of several "sharp business practices" by which the insurer is sometimes defrauded of his insurance, and especially has he read of new methods and cheap plans of insurance. He suggests that it would be well to change this and that policy to another and very solid old company. You see, gentlemen, the business man of this day has to read, yes, and study, and go to the roots of many things, that he may avoid the pitfalls that surround business upon every side. He would not be an employer worth having that did not note what kind of a young man that was, although now in the humble guise of a clerk.

The Second Step Upward.

Suppose he is an electrician or engineer, and comes from Sibley, which is a good place to come from. In the great manufacturing concern so fortunate as to secure his services, he has to do with some humble branch of the work, but he discovers that there are a few boilers which are not quite safe, and that the engines or motors are built upon false mechanical principles, and are very wasteful of fuel, and that one of the engines will soon give trouble; there is a foundation under it upon which he finds that the contractor has not done honest work; or dropping into the works one night just to see that all is going well, perhaps he discovers that a man trusted by the firm has fallen into bad habits, and is not fit for duty, or perhaps is not on duty, and that an accident might thus happen. He feels it to be his duty to take action here and safeguard the business from the danger of an accident. He draws the plans which show some defects in the machinery, lays them before his employers with suggestions how to cure these, made upon the latest scientific principles that he had been taught in Sibley. The employer, of course, is very averse to spend money, and angry to learn that his machinery is not what it should be. But although his anger explodes and envelops the young man for a moment, he is not shooting at him; when the debris clears off he sits down and learns from the young man what a few thousand dollars now might save, and the result is that he tells the Sibley boy he wishes him to take up this subject and attend to it, and be sure to make it all right.

Already that young man's fortune is almost as good as made. He could not hide his light under a bushel if he tried, and the coming business man is not excessively liable to that sin, and does not want to; he is business all over There is no affectation or false modesty about him. He knows his business, and he feels fully conscious and proud of the fact that he knows it, and that is one of the many advantages Sibley gives him, and he is determined that his employer should not, at least upon that point, know less than he does. You must never fail to enlighten your employer. You cannot keep such a young man as that back; and this let me tell you, no employer wishes to keep him back. There is only one person as happy at finding this young man as the young man is in finding himself, and that is his employer. He is worth a million, more or less, but, of course, it would not be good for him to get it while so young.

He has now made two steps forward. First, he has got a start, and, secondly, he has satisfied his employer that he renders exceptional service, a decisive step; as the French say, "he has arrived," and is there to stay. His foot is upon the ladder; how high he climbs is his own affair. He is among the few within the very threshold of the whole business.

There is a good deal to be done after this, however. This

young man has zeal and ability, and he has shown that he
has also that indispensable quality—judgment; and he has
shown another indispensable quality—that his heart is in
the business; that no other cause takes him from it; that he
pushes aside the very seductive temptations which surround
young men, and concentrates his attention, his time, his
efforts, upon the performance of his duties to his employer.
All other studies, occupations, and all amusements are sub-
ordinate to the business, which holds paramount sway. His
salary, of course, increases. If he has happened to engage
with an employer who does not fully appreciate such services as he has rendered, and is ready to render, other employers have not failed to note that here is that rare article,
the exceptional young man, in the service of their rival, and
it is possible that our young hero may have to change employers. It does not often happen, but it does sometimes,
that a young man has to do so. As a rule, the employer is
only too thankful that such a young man has come to him,
and he makes it his interest to remain. Confidence is a
matter of slow growth, however, and it is a far cry from a
high salary as a hireling, into equality as a partner.

The Crucial Question.

Let us trace him a little further. This young man's
services to the firm have been such as to render it necessary
some day that he should visit his employer at his house.
It is not long before many occasions arise which call the
young man to the house, where he is now favored upon his
merits by the household, and to whom his nature soon becomes known, and the master soon begins to ask himself
whether he might not some day make him a partner, and
then comes the question of questions: **Is he honest** and
true? Let me pause here one moment.

Gentlemen, this is the crucial question, the keystone of
the arch; for no amount of ability is of the slightest avail
without honor. When Burns pictured the Genius of Scotland in "The Vision," these marvelous words came to him:

"Her eye, ev'n turn'd on empty space,
Beam'd keen wi' honor."

No concealment, no prevarication, no speculation, trying to win something for which no service is given; nothing done which, if published, would involve your shame. The business man seeks first in his partner "the soul of honor," one who would swerve from the narrow path even to serve him would only forfeit his confidence. Is he intelligent? Is he capable of forming a correct judgment, based upon knowledge, upon distant and far-reaching issues? Young men, yes, and old men also, sometimes marry in haste, which is very foolish in both cases. But there is this to be said for the partnership—it is rarely entered upon in a hurry. It is not one or two qualities which insure it, but an all-around character, desirable in many respects, highly objectionable in none, and with special ability in one or two.

We often hear in our day that it is impossible for young men to become owners, because business is conducted upon so great a scale that the capital necessary reaches millions, and, therefore, the young man is doomed to a salaried life. Now there is something in that view only so far as the great corporations are concerned, because an interest in these is only obtainable by capital; you can buy so many shares for so many dollars, and as the class of young men I address are not willing to remain forever salaried men, but are determined sooner or later, to become business men upon their own account, as masters, I do not believe that employment in a great corporation is as favorable for them as with private owners, because, while a young man can look forward to a large salary in their service, that is all to which he can aspire. Even the presidents of these corporations, being only salaried men, are not to be classed as strictly business men at all. How, then, can a young man under them be anything but a salaried man his life long?

Where to Look for Opportunities.

Many a business which has long been successful as a partnership is put into a joint stock concern, and the shares are offered in the market, and professional men, guilelessly innocent of business, and, sometimes, women of a

speculative turn, and, I am sorry to say, many times clergy-
men, and artists, are deluded into purchasing. The public buys the business, but they should have bought the
man or men who made the business.

You remember the Travers story? A friend called Travers in to see a dog that he wished to buy to clear his
conservatory of rats, and when the dog-fancier undertook
to show him how this dog demolished these pests, one
great, big old rat chased the dog. Travers' friend said to
him:

"What would you do?"

Travers replied: "B-b-b-buy the rat."

The public often buys the wrong thing.

It would be an excellent study for you to read frequently the stock-lists of miscellaneous companies. You will
find some of the newspapers give the list, and then note the
par value of the shares and the price at which you may
purchase them. It may be said that this par value is upon
fictitious capital. That is so only in some instances; in
manufacturing companies especially, I think the reverse is
the rule. The capital does not fully represent the cost of
the properties.

But there are many corporations which are not corporations, many instances of partnership in which the corporate
form has been adopted, and yet the business continued
substantially as a partnership, and comparing such institutions with the great corporations whose ownership is
here, there, and everywhere, we find a most notable difference. Take, for instance, the great steamship lines of
the world. Most of these, as those of you who read well
know, fail to make returns to their shareholders. The
shares of some of the greatest companies have been selling
at one-half and sometimes one-third -their cost. These
are corporations, pure and simple, but if we look at other

lines engaged upon the same oceans, which are managed by their owners and in which, generally, one great business man is deeply interested and at the head, we find large dividends each year and amounts placed to the reserve fund. It is the difference between individualism and communism applied to business, between the owners managing their own business as partners, and a joint stock concern of a thousand shifting owners ignorant of the business.

The same contrast can be drawn in every branch of business, in merchandising, in manufacturing, in finance, in transportation by land as well as by sea. It is so with banks. Many banks are really the property of a few business men. These soon become the leading banks, and their shares are invariably quoted at the highest premium, especially if the president of the bank be the largest owner, as he is in many of the most remarkable cases of success. In such partnership corporations there is every opportunity for the coming business man to obtain ownership which exists in pure partnerships, for the owners of both manage affairs and are on the constant watch for ability.

Do not be fastidious; take what the gods offer. Begin, if necessary, with a corporation, always keeping your eye open for a chance to become interested in a business of your own. Remember every business can be made successful, because it supplies some essential want of the community; it performs a needed office, whether it be in manufacturing which produces an article, or in gathering and distributing it by the merchant; or the banker, whose business is to take care of an invest capital.

There is no line of business in which success is not attainable.

A Secret of Success.

It is a simple matter of honest work, ability, and concentration. There is no question about there being room at the top for exceptional men in any profession. These have not to seek patronage; the question is, rather, how can their services be secured, and, as with every profession, so in every line of business, there is plenty of room at the top. Your problem is how to get there. The answer is simple: conduct your business with just a little more ability than the average man in your line. If you are only above the average your success is secured, and the degree of success is in ratio to the greater degree of ability and attention which you give above the average. There are always a few in business who stand near the top, but there are always an infinitely greater number at or near the bottom. And should you fail to ascend, the fault is not in your stars, but in yourselves. Those who fail may say that this or that man had great advantages, the fates were propitious, the conditions favorable. Now, there is very little in this; one man lands in the middle of the stream which he tries to jump, and is swept away, and another tries the same feat, and lands upon the other side.

Examine these two men.

You will find that the one who failed lacked judgment; he had not calculated the means to the end; was a foolish fellow; had not trained himself; could not jump; he took the chances. He was like the young lady who was asked if she could play the violin; she said she "did not know, she had never tried." Now, the other man who jumped the stream had carefully trained himself; he knew about how far he could jump, and there was one thing "dead sure" with him, he knew he could, at any rate, jump far enough to land at a point from which he could wade ashore, and try again. He had shown judgment.

Prestige is a great matter, my friends. A young man who has the record of doing what he sets out to do will find year after year his field of operations extended, and the tasks committed to him greater and greater. On the other hand, the man who has to admit failure and comes to friends trying to get assistance in order to make a second start is in a very bad position, indeed.

College Graduates in Business.

The graduates of our colleges and universities in former years graduated while yet in their teens. We have changed this, and graduates are older, as a rule, when they enter upon life's struggle, but they are taught much more. Unless the young university man employs his time to the very best advantage in acquiring knowledge upon the pursuit which he is to make the chief business of his life, he will enter business at a disadvantage with younger men who enter in their teens, although lacking in university education. This goes without saying. Now, the question is: Will the graduate who has dwelt in the region of theory overtake the man who has been for a year or two in advance of him, engaged in the hard and stern educative field of practice.)

That it is possible for the graduate to do so also goes without saying, and that he should in after life possess views broader than the ordinary business man, deprived of university education, is also certain, and, of course, the race in life is to those whose record is best at the end; the beginning is forgotten and is of no moment. But if the graduate is ever to overtake the first starter in the race, it must be by possessing stronger staying-powers; his superior knowledge leading to sounder judgment must be depended upon to win the race at the finish. A few disadvantages he must strenuously guard against, the lack of severe self-discipline, of strenuous concentration, and intense ambition, which usually characterizes the man who starts before the habits of manhood are formed. The habits of the young man at college, after he is a man, and the habits of the youngster in the business arena are likely to differ.

There is another great disadvantage which the older man has to overcome in most successful business establishments. There will be found in operation there a strict civil-service system and promotion without favor. It is, therefore, most difficult to find admission to the service in any but the lowest grades. One has to begin at the foot, and this is better for all parties concerned, especially the young graduate.

The exceptional graduate should excel the exceptional non-graduate. He has more education, and education will always tell, the other qualities being equal. Take two men of equal natural ability, energy, and the same ambition and characteristics, and the man who has received the best, widest, most suitable education has the advantage over the other, undoubtedly.

Business Men and Speculators.

All pure coins have their counterfeits; the counterfeit of business is speculation. A man in business always gives value in return for his revenue, and thus performs a useful function. His services are necessary and benefit the community; besides, he labors steadily in developing the resources of the country, and thus contributes to the advancement of the race. This is genuine coin. Speculation, on the contrary, is a parasite fastened upon the labor of business men. It creates nothing and supplies no want. When the speculator wins he takes money without rendering service, or giving value therefor, and when he loses, his fellow-speculator takes the money from him. It is a pure gambling operation between them, degrading to both. You can never be an honest man of business and a speculator. The modes and aims of the one career are fatal to the other. No business man can honestly speculate, for those who trust him have a right to expect strict adherence to business methods. The creditor takes the usual risks of business, but not those of speculation. The genuine and the counterfeit have nothing in common.

That 95 per cent fail of those who start in business upon their own account seems incredible, and yet such are said to be the statistics upon the subject. Although it is said that figures will say anything, still it is a fact that the proportion is very great. Do not think that I wish to discourage you against attempting to be your own masters and having a business of your own; very far from it. Besides, the coming business man is not to be discouraged by anything that anybody can say. He is a true knight who says with Fitzjames:

"If the path be dangerous known,
The danger self is lure alone."

The young man who is determined to be a business man will not be thwarted, neither will he be diverted into any other channel, and he is going to start and have a trial; he will "make a spoon or spoil a horn" trying to make it. He must go ahead and find it out. Time enough to confine yourself to a life-long bondage as mere receivers of a salary after you have tried business, and really discovered whether or not you are one of the gifted who possess all the necessary qualities.

I have tried to sketch the path of the exceptional graduate from salary to partnership. It is no fancy sketch; there is not a day passes without changes in many firms which raise young men to partnership, and in every single city no first of January passes without such promotions. Business requires fresh young blood for its existence. If any of you are discouraged upon this point, let me give you two stories within my own experience, which should certainly cheer you.

A Sketch from Life.

There is a large manufacturer, the largest in the world in his line. I know him well, a splendid man, who illustrates the business career at its best. Now, like all sensible business men, as he grew in years he realized that fresh blood must be introduced into his business; that while it was comparatively easy for him to manage the extensive business at present, it was wise to provide for its continuance in able hands after he had retired. Rich men seldom have sons who inherit a taste for business. I am not concerned to say whether this is well or otherwise. Looking at the human race as a whole, I believe it is for good.

If rich men's sons had poor men's necessities, and, hence their ambitious abilities, there would be less chance for the students of colleges than there is. It was not to any member of his family that this man looked for the new young blood. A young man in the service of a corporation had attracted his attention in the management of certain business matters connected with the firm. The young man had to call upon this gentleman frequently. The wise man did not move hastily in the matter. About his ability he was soon satisfied, but that covered only one point of many. What were the young man's surroundings, habits, tastes, acquirements? Beyond his immediate business, what was his nature? He found everything in these matters just as he would have it. The young man was supporting a widowed mother and a sister; he had as friends some excellent young men, and some older than himself; he was a student; he was a reader; had high tastes, of course; I need hardly say that he was a young gentleman, highly self-respecting, the soul of honor, incapable of anything low or vulgar; in short, a model young man, and of course, poor—that goes without saying.

The young man was sent for, and the millionaire told him that he should like very much to try him in his service, and asked the young man if he would make the trial. The millionaire stated frankly what he was looking for—a young business man who might develop, and finally relieve him of much care. The arrangement was that he should come for two years as a clerk, subject to clerk's rules, which in this case was very hard, because he had to be at the factory a few minutes before seven in the morning. He was to have a salary somewhat larger than he had received, and, if at the end of two years nothing had been said on either side, no obligations were weaved, each was free. He was simply on trial. The young man proudly said he would not have it otherwise.

The business went on. Before the two years expired the employer was satisfied that he had found that exceedingly rare thing, a young business man. What a number of qualities this embraces, including judgment, for without judgment a business man amounts to nothing. The employer stated to the young man that he was delighted with him, pleased with his services, and expressed his joy at having found him. He had now arranged to interest him in the firm. But to his amazement the young man replied:

"Thanks, thanks, but it is impossible for me to accept."

"What is the matter? You suit me; do I not suit you?"

"Excuse me, sir, but for reasons which I cannot explain, I am to leave your service in six months, when my two years are up, and I intended to give you notice of this, that you might fill my place."

"Where are you going?"

"I am going abroad."

"Have you made any engagement?"

"No, sir."

"Do you not know where you are going?"

"No, sir."

"Nor what you are to do?"

"No, sir."

"Sir, I have treated you well, and I do think I am entitled to know the real reason. I think it is your duty to tell me."

The reason was dragged out of the young man. "You have been too good to me. I would give anything to be able to remain with you. You even invited me to your house; you have been absent traveling; you asked me to call often to take your wife and daughter to such entertainments as they wished to attend, and I cannot stand it any longer."

Well, the millionaire, of course, discovered what all of you have suspected, just what you would have done under the circumstances. He had fallen in love with the daughter. Now in this country that would not have been considered much of an indiscretion, and I do not advise any of you to fight against it. If you really love, you should overlook the objection that it is your employer's daughter who has conquered, and that you may have to bear the burden of riches; but in the land of which I speak it would have been considered dishonorable for a young clerk to make love to any young lady without the parents' permission.

"Have you spoken to my daughter?" was the question. The young man scarcely deigned to reply to that.

"Of course not."

"Never said a word, or led her to suspect in any way?"

"Of course not."

"Well," he said, "I do not see why you should not; you are the very kind of son-in-law I want if you can win my daughter."

Very strange, but somehow or other, the young lady did not differ from papa; he was the kind of husband she wanted. Now that young man is a happy business man today.

Romance in Business

I have another story which happened in another country. Both the fathers-in-law told me these stories themselves, and proud men they are, and proud am I of their friendship. You see, business is not all this hard prosaic life that it is pictured. It bears romance and sentiment in it, and the greater the business, the more successful, the more useful, in my experience, there is found the more romance and imagination. The highest triumphs even in business flow from romance, sentiment, imagination, particularly in the business of a world-wide firm.

The other story is so similar to the first that successful telling is impossible. You will all jump to the conclusion, and the details in these cases are nothing. It is as when I began to tell my young nephews about the battle of Bannockburn; there were the English, and there stood the Scotch.

"Which whipped, uncle?" cried the three at once—details unnecessary. But there was no battle in this case. I infer it was all settled by amicable arbitration.

I shall not tell it at length, as I did the other, but it is precisely the same, except that the young man in this case was not employed except in the ordinary manner. The young man's services were needed, and he was employed. He finally became private secretary to the millionaire, and with equally fatal results. In this case, however, the father asked the exemplary and able young man to look after his sons during his absence. This necessitated visits to the residence at the country house, and sports and games with the sons. My friend forgot he had a daughter, and he should not have done this. When you become not only heads of business but heads of families, you should make a note of this, and not think your sons everything. The private secretary, who was requested to attend to the sons, somehow or other, getting his instructions verbally, seems to have understood them as having a slightly wider range. The daughter apparently needed most of his attention. But note this: These two young men won the confidence and captured the judgment and admiration of their employers—business men—first, and then fell in love with the daughters. You will be perfectly safe if you take matters in the same order of precedence.

Value of a Business Career.

Perhaps I may be permitted, without going too far beyond the scope of my text, to make a few remarks upon the influence of a business career upon men, as compared with other pursuits.

First, then, I have learned that the artistic career is most narrowing, and produces such petty jealousies, unbounded vanities, and spitefulness, as to furnish me with a great contrast to that which I have found in men of affairs. Music, painting, sculpture, one would think, should prove most powerful in their beneficent effects upon those who labor with them as their daily vocation. Experience, however, is against this. Perhaps, because the work, or the performance, of artists is so highly personal, so clearly seen, being brought directly before the public, that petty passions are stimulated; however that may be, I believe it will not be controverted that the artistic mind becomes prejudiced and narrow. But, understand, I speak only of classes and of the general effect; everywhere we find exceptions which render the average still more satisfactory. In regard to what are called the learned professions, we notice the effect produced by specialization in a very marked degree.

In the ministerial class this is not so marked in our day, because leaders in that great function permit themselves a wider range of subjects than ever before, and are dealing less with creeds and formulas and more and more with the practical evils and shortcomings of human life in its various phases. This naturally broadens the mind. It has been held that the legal profession must tend to make clear. but narrow, intellects, and it is pointed out that great lawyers have seldom arisen to commanding position and power over their fellows. This does not mean that men who study law become unsatisfactory legislators or statesmen and rulers. If it did, our country, of all others, should be in a bady way, because we are governed by lawyers. But the most famous Americans who have been great men were not great lawyers; that is, they have seldom attained the foremost rank in the profession, but have availed themselves of the inestimable advantage which the study of law confers upon a statesman, and developed beyond the bounds of the profession. We are reminded that the great lawyer and the great judge must deal with rules and precedents already established; the lawyer follows precedents, but the ruler of men makes precedents.

Merchants and Professional Men.

The tendency of all professions, it would seem, must be to make what is known as the professional mind clear, but narrow. Now what may be claimed for business as a career is that the man in business is called upon to deal with an ever-changing variety of questions. He must have an all-round judgment based upon knowledge of many subjects.

It is not sufficient for the great merchant and business man
of our day that he know his country well, its physical
conditions, its resources, statistics, crops, waterways, its
finances, in short, all conditions which affect not only the
present, but which give him data upon which he can pre-
dict, with some degree of certainty, the future.

The merchant whose operations extend to various countries must also know these countries, and also the chief
things pertaining to them. His view must be world-wide;
nothing can happen of moment which has not its bearing
upon his action—political complications at Constantinople;
the appearance of the cholera in the East; monsoon in In-
dia; the supply of gold at Cripple Creek; the appearance of
the Colorado beetle or the fall of a ministry; the danger of
war; the likelihood of arbitration compelling settlement—
nothing can happen in any part of the world which he has
not to consider. He must possess one of the rarest qualities—be an excellent judge of men; he often employs
thousands, and knows how to bring the best out of various
characters; he must have the gift of organization—another
rare gift; must have executive ability; must be able to de-
cide promptly and wisely.

Now, none of these rare qualities are so absolutely essential to the specialist in any branch or profession. He follows a career, therefore, which tends not only to sharpen
his wits, but to enlarge his powers; different, also, from
any other careers, that it tends not to specialization and
the working of the mind within narrow grooves, but tends
to develop in a man capacity to judge upon wide data. No
professional life embraces so many problems, none other
requires so wide a view of affairs in general. I think,
therefore, that it may justly be said, for the business
career, that it must widen and develop the intellectual powers of its devotee.

On the other hand, the professional career is immeasur-
ably nobler in this: that it has not for its chief end the
ignoble aim of money-making and is free from the greatest

danger which besets the career of business, which is in one
sense the most sordid of all careers if entered upon in the
wrong spirit. To make money is no doubt the primary consideration with most young men who enter it. I think
if you will look into your hearts you will finds this to be
true. But while this may be the first, it should not be the
last consideration.

There is the great use which a man can perform in developing the resources of his country; in furnishing employment to thousands; in developing inventions which
prove of great benefit to the race, to help it forward. The
successful man of affairs soon rises above the mere desire
to make money as the chief end of his labors; that is super-
seded by thoughts of the uses he performs in the line which
I have just mentioned. The merchant soon finds his strong-
est feeling to be that of pride in the extent of his interna-
tional operations; in his ships sailing every sea. The manufacturer finds in his employees, and in his works, in machinery, in improvements, in the perfection of his factories
and methods his chief interest and reward. The profitable
return they make is chiefly acceptable not because this is
mere money, but because it denotes success.

There is a romantic as well as prosaic side to business.
The young man who begins in a financial firm and deals with
capital invested in a hundred different ways—in bonds
upon our railway systems, in money lent to the merchant
and to the manufacturer to enable them to work their wonders—soon finds romance in business and unlimited room
for the imagination. He can furnish credit world-wide in
its range. His simple letter will carry the traveler to the
farthest part of the earth. He may even be of service to
his country in a crisis, as Richard Morris, the great merchant in Philadelphia, was to General Washington in the
Revolutionary cause, or, as in our own day, our great bank-
ers have been in providing gold to our Government at several crises to avert calamity.

The Vanished Prejudice Against Trade.

If the young man does not find romance in his business, it is not the fault of the business, but the fault of the young man. Consider the wonders, the mysteries connected with the recent developments in that most spiritual of all agents —electricity—with its unknown, and, perhaps, even unguessed-of powers. He must be a dull and prosaic young man who, being connected with electricity in any of its forms, is not lifted from humdrum business to the region of the mysterious. Business is not all dollars; these are but the shell—the kernel lies within and is to be enjoyed later, as the higher faculties of the business man, so constantly called into play, develop and mature. There was in the reign of militarism and barbarous force much contempt for the man who engaged in trade. How completely has all this changed! But, indeed, the feeling was of recent origin, for if we look further back we find the oldest families in the world proud of nothing but the part they played in business. The woolsack and the galley still flourish in their coat-of-arms. One of the most—perhaps the most—influential statesmen in England in 1896 was the Duke of Devonshire—because he had the confidence of both parties. He was the president of the Barrow Steel Company. The members of the Conservative cabinet were found to hold sixty-four directorships in various trading, manufacturing and mining companies. In Britain today not how to keep out of trade, but how to get into it, is the question. The late President of the French Republic, a man with a marvelous career, had been a business man all his days. The old feeling of aversion has entirely gone.

You remember that the late Emperor of Germany wished to make his friend, the steel manufacturer, Krupp, a Prince of the empire, but that business man was too proud of his works, and the son of his father, and begged the Emperor to excuse him from degrading the rank he held as King of Steel.

The old prejudice against trade has gone even from the strongholds in Europe. This change has come because trade itself has changed. In old days every branch of business was conducted upon the smallest retail scale, and small dealings in small affairs breed small men; besides, every man had to be occupied with the details, and, indeed, each man manufactured or traded for himself. The higher qualities of organization and of enterprise, of broad views and of executive ability, were not brought into play. In our day, business in all branches is conducted upon so gigantic a scale that partners of a huge concern are rulers over a domain. The large employer of labor sometimes has more men in his industrial army than the petty German kings had under their banners.

It was said of old that two of a trade never agree; today the warmest friendships are formed in every department of human effort among those in the same business; each visits the other's counting-house, factory, warehouse; they are shown the different methods; all the improvements; new inventions, and freely adapt them to their own business.

Affairs are now too great to breed petty jealousies, and there is now allied with the desire for gain the desire for progress, invention, improved methods, scientic development, and pride of success in these important matters; so that the dividend which the business man seeks and receives today, is not alone in dollars. He receives with the dollar something better, a dividend in the shape of satisfaction in being instrumental in carrying forward to higher stages of development the business which he makes his life-work.

Rewards of a Business Career.

I can confidently recommend to you the business career as one in which there is abundant room for the exercise of man's highest power, and of every good quality in human nature. I believe the career of the great merchant, or banker, or captain of industry, to be favorable to the development of the powers of the mind, and to the ripening of the judgment upon a wide range of general subjects; to freedom from prejudice, and the keeping of an open mind. And I do know that permanent success is not obtainable except by fair and honorable dealing, by irreproachable habits and correct living, by the display of good sense and rare judgment in all the relations of human life, for credit and confidence fly from the business man, foolish in word and deed, or irregular in habits, or even suspected of sharp practice. There may be room for a foolish man in every profession—foolish as a child beyond the range of his specialty, and yet successful in that—but no man ever saw a foolish business man successful. If without sound, all-round judgment, he must fail.

The business career is thus a stern school of all the virtues, and there is one supreme reward which it often yields which no other career can promise; I point to noble benefactions which it renders possible. It is to business men following business careers that we chiefly owe our universities, colleges, libraries, and educational institutions, as witness Girard, Lehigh, Chicago, Harvard, Yale, Cornell and many others.

What monument can a man leave behind him productive of so much good and so certain to hand his name down to succeeding generations, hallowed with the blessings of thousands in each decade who have within its walls received that most precious possession, a sound and liberal education? These are the works of men who recognized that surplus wealth was a sacred trust, to be administered during the life of its possessor for the highest good of his fellows.

If, then, some business man may fall subject to the reproach of grasping, we can justly claim for them as a class what honest Thomas Cromwell claimed for the great cardinal, and say: "If they have a greed of getting, yet in bestowing they are most princely, as witness these seats of learning."

CPSIA information can be obtained at www.ICGtesting.com
Printed in the USA
LVOW10s1015080716

495623LV00019B/254/P